All you need to know

2 Peter

by

Bryson Smith

The Good Book Company
Elm House, 37 Elm Road
New Malden, Surrey KT3 3HB, UK
Tel: 020-8942-0880; Fax: 020-8942-0990
e-mail: admin@thegoodbook.co.uk
www.thegoodbook.co.uk

ISBN 1-873166-07-9

Contents

How to make the most of these studies

1. What is an Interactive Bible Study?

These 'interactive' Bible studies are a bit like a guided tour of a famous city. The studies will take you through Peter's letter, pointing out things along the way, filling in background details, and suggesting avenues for further exploration. But there is also time for you to do some sight-seeing of your own—to wander off, have a good look for yourself, and form your own conclusions.

In other words, we have designed these studies to fall halfway between a sermon and a set of unadorned Bible study questions. We want to provide stimulation and input and point you in the right direction, while leaving you to do a lot of the exploration and discovery yourself.

We hope that these studies will stimulate lots of 'interaction'—interaction with the Bible, with the things we've written, with your own current thoughts and attitudes, with other people as you discuss them, and with God as you talk to him about it all.

2. The Format

Each study contains sections of text to introduce, summarize, suggest and provoke. We've left plenty of room in the margins for you to jot comments and questions as you read. Interspersed throughout the text are two types of 'interaction', each with their own symbol:

Investigate

Questions to help you investigate key parts of the Bible.

Think it Through

Questions to help you think through the implications of your discoveries and write down your own thoughts and reactions.

When you come to one of these symbols, you'll know that it's time to do some work of your own.

3. Suggestions for Individual Study

- Before you begin, pray that God would open your eyes to what he is saying in 2 Peter and give you the spiritual strength to do something about it. You may be spurred to pray again at the end of the study.
- Work through the study, following the directions as you go. Write in the spaces provided.
- Resist the temptation to skip over the *think it through* sections. It is important to think about the sections of text (rather than just accepting them as true) and to ponder the implications for your life. Writing these things down is a very valuable way to get your thoughts working.
- Take what opportunities you can to talk to others about what you've learnt.

4. Suggestions for Group Study

- Much of the above applies to group study as well. The studies are suitable for structured Bible study or cell groups, as well as for more informal pairs and three-somes. Get together with a friend/s and work through them at your own pace. You don't need the formal structure of a 'group' to gain maximum benefit.
- It is *vital* that group members work through the study themselves *before* the group meets. The group discussion can take place comfortably in an hour (depending on how side-tracked you get!), but only if all the members have done the work and are familiar with the material.
- Spend most of the group time discussing the 'interactive' sections—investigate and think it through. Reading all the text together will take too long and should be unnec-essary if the group members have done their preparation. You may wish to underline and read aloud particular paragraphs or sections of text that you think are impor-tant.
- The role of the group leader is to direct the course of the discussion and to try to draw the threads together at the end. This will mean a little extra preparation—underlin-ing important sections of text to emphasize, working out which questions are worth concentrating on, and being

sure of the main thrust of the study. Leaders will also probably want to work out approximately how long they'd like to spend on each part.

- We haven't included an 'answer guide' to the questions in the studies. This is a deliberate move. We want to give you a guided tour of 2 Peter, not a lecture. There is more than enough in the text we have written and the questions we have asked to point you in what we think is the right direction. The rest is up to you. (If you *would* like some additional input, there is a series of tapes available that expound the relevant passages. For details, see the pages inside the back cover.)

The finish line

The first woman to swim the English Channel both ways was Florence Chadwick. Her next challenge was to swim from Catalina Island to mainland California, a distance of over 30km.

After 15 hours of swimming, Florence Chadwick was pulled out of the water, exhausted, just 800 metres from her goal.

Why couldn't she make that final effort and fulfil her ambition? The answer lies in the weather: it was a foggy day, and Florence couldn't see the shore. She didn't know how close she was.

Two months later, on a clear day, she swam all the way.

Seeing the finish line makes all the difference to an athlete; it provides new energy and fresh motivation. But when the end is nowhere in sight, it's very hard to keep going.

This fact has not been lost on the apostle Peter. In 2 Peter, the apostle writes to show his readers the finish line.

In this short epistle Peter writes to Christians like us: Christians who are being buffeted by false teachers; Christians who are struggling to live holy lives; Christians who are being ridiculed about their beliefs. Peter writes to urge them to press on and to think clearly about their faith. Peter does that by reminding them and us of the glorious goal that we have to look forward to in the eternal kingdom of our Lord and Saviour Jesus Christ. If we keep this goal in mind it will provide the motivation for us to keep going. If we keep this goal in mind it will help us to be clear-thinking Christians.

An overview

One of the nicest things about 2 Peter is that it is short. You can easily read the whole thing in one sitting. In fact, that is exactly the best way to start studying it.

Investigate

1. *Read through all of 2 Peter.* What is your overall impression of the letter? Is it a happy letter? A sad letter? An angry letter?

2. Now skim back through the letter and answer the following questions.

The author

What information can you discover about the author of 2 Peter?

How does he describe himself?

What is his situation at the time of writing?

Why is he writing?

The audience

What can you discover about the original recipients of the letter?

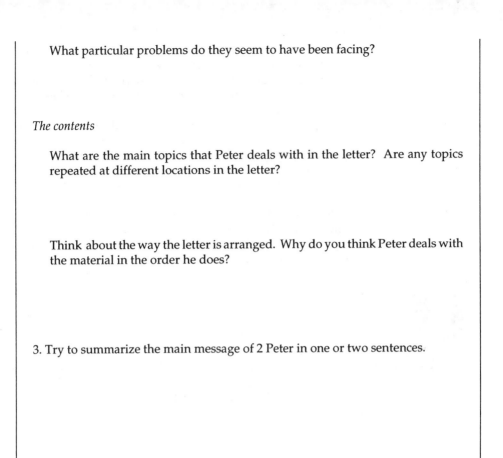

What particular problems do they seem to have been facing?

The contents

What are the main topics that Peter deals with in the letter? Are any topics repeated at different locations in the letter?

Think about the way the letter is arranged. Why do you think Peter deals with the material in the order he does?

3. Try to summarize the main message of 2 Peter in one or two sentences.

A dying man's wish

The self-confessed reason for Peter's writing is that he wants to stimulate his readers to clear "wholesome" thinking (3:1). In particular, Peter wants his readers to have accurate knowledge about Jesus.

This is no better seen than in 1:12-15. In those verses Peter explains that he hasn't much longer to live. He describes this in terms of soon putting aside the "tent of this body". This has caused many people to speculate that Peter was writing this letter from death row in a Roman prison. Tradition has it that Peter was crucified upside down in Rome, although solid historical evidence is scant.

Whatever the exact circumstances, what is significant is that Peter's dying wish is that people are firmly established in Jesus. So important is it for people to have a correct knowledge of Jesus that Peter wants to spend his last dying days making sure that they are solidly grounded in a true knowledge of Jesus.

This is because Peter has a clear view of the Christian finish line. Peter knows that there is more to this life than this life. This is reflected in the way he refers to his earthly body as a tent (1:13). The very image of a tent conveys the feeling of something temporary. You might pitch a tent for a short time on holidays, but it's not really a long-term dwelling. Peter's point is that our earthly bodies are not long-term dwellings. He knows that as followers of Jesus, we look forward to our heavenly bodies, beyond that glorious finishing line.

Because of this eternal perspective on life, Peter appreciates how critical it is to have a clear understanding of Jesus. As we will discover, it is this theme of being clear-minded about Christ that lies at the heart of the letter.

Think it through

1. Imagine you had a short time to live. What are the things you would like to fill your last days with? How does your thinking compare with Peter's?

2. Peter wants his readers to be firmly established in the truth of Jesus. What specific things can we do to establish ourselves in the truth?

3. It is sometimes said that you can be so heavenly minded that you're of no earthly use. Do you think that this is true? How might Peter respond to such a saying?

4. It can sometimes be a little depressing when we compare ourselves to people like Peter. He is so motivated and clear-minded about the gospel. How do the following passages encourage us?

James 1:2-5

Romans 8:26-30

Philippians 3:10-16

Know where you're going

Being a Christian is more like hopping into a railway carriage than getting behind the wheel of a car. The train goes in a particular direction, guided by the tracks. Its destination and its stops along the way are clear. A car, on the other hand, can go anywhere you wish—your destination is yours to control.

In the first chapter of his letter, Peter talks about where the Christians's life is going and what we can expect to happen along the way. Peter shows us the goals and ambitions appropriate to those who "have received a faith as precious as ours" (1:1).

Investigate

Read 2 Peter 1:1-4

1. What privileges do we enjoy as Christians?

2. What do these verses say about how we obtain these privileges?

3. What things does the world think you need to be equipped for life? What does Peter think you need?

4. What do you think it means to participate in the divine nature? How does this relate to escaping from the corruption of the world? (These verses might help: 2 Cor 3:17-18; 1 Pet 5:1; 1 Jn 3:1-2.)

The Christian start

We have only gone four verses into the epistle, but already Peter is saying earth-shattering things. Peter is sharing how unimaginably important a knowledge of Jesus is in this life. Knowledge of Jesus will give you everything you need for life. Through a knowledge of Jesus we become enmeshed with the God of all the universe who helps us "escape the corruption in the world caused by evil desires". In other words, it is by knowing about Jesus that we enter such an intimate relationship with God that his Spirit dwells in us and transforms us.

Notice in all this that God gives us all we *need* through a knowledge of Jesus (1:3). He doesn't give us all that we might *want*. In our sinful state, there is much that we want in the world but which God in his wisdom considers that we are better off without.

However, all this is really only the beginning. It's not a matter of simply receiving these privileges offered to us in Jesus and then sitting back with our feet up. We have to work out our knowledge of Jesus in our daily behaviour. Peter, therefore, offers direction about how we should live once we've started with all the privileges that come through a knowledge of Jesus Christ.

Investigate

Read 1:5-9

1. List the things that Peter says we should build into our Christian lives. How is each of these qualities important?

2. What is the end result of adding the above things to our lives?

3. What might it mean to be effective and productive in our Lord Jesus Christ? (See also Col 1:9-12; Jas 2:14-17.)

The Christian life

In verses 5-7, Peter catalogues seven important aspects of Christian living. Roll them all up and Peter is telling us to be working hard at our Christian life. We are not just to fill our heads with knowledge of Jesus. We are to live out that knowledge in our behaviour. There is no point in just reading verses 5-7. We must act on them, and if we don't we are being slack Christians. We are blind to what Jesus has done for us and we are unfruitful for God.

Investigate

Read 1:10-11

1. If we do the things Peter suggests in verses 5-7, what will we have to look forward to?

2. What does it mean "to make your calling sure"? (You may need to come back to this question after reading more of the letter.)

The Christian finish

Picture the scene at the Olympics when the marathon event is coming to an end and the leader first runs into the stadium. We've all seen—at least on television—the crowd rise to its feet and heard that deafening cheer which fills the arena. What an adrenalin rush that would be—to be that runner and to hear the crowd!

Peter says that we will be like that runner if we make every effort to supplement our faith. Heaven will rise to its feet as we enter. We will have finished the race with honour. We will have lived fruitful lives for Jesus and we will have been effective and productive in our knowledge of Jesus. 2 Peter is revolutionary in the way that, through images such as these, it stretches our horizons to God's horizons. Sometimes we get caught in our own little corridor of life and petty things grow out of all perspective. Life becomes dominated by the TV guide or the house and garden or our sport or career.

God is concerned with bigger things than those. God is concerned about eternity and heaven and hell. When you take that big picture into consideration, many of the things that we think are important actually aren't important at all. In fact, some of the things that we might be a bit too causal and flippant about, like knowledge of Jesus, turn into the most important things of all!

Peter, therefore, does us a great service as he opens his letter. He reminds us of the importance of a knowledge of Jesus. Knowledge of Jesus gives us everything we need for life, and therefore we should be working hard at living that knowledge out in actions so that we can enjoy a rich welcome into the eternal kingdom of our Lord and Saviour Jesus Christ.

Think it through

1. Think of the things you consider most important in your life. How important are they from the perspective of eternity?

2. List three areas in your life where you would consider yourself to be an effective and productive Christian?

3. Look down the list Peter gives in verses 5-7 and pick at least one area which you think needs specific work in your own life. What are some ways that you can 'increase your measure' of that quality during this week?

4. Why is it so easy to be distracted from our heavenly goal?

5. Consider Jesus' words in Matthew 6:19-34. Where are you storing treasure?

The importance of being right

Sometimes, there is no substitute for being right.

The surgeon has to be certain that the correct blood vessel is clamped before cutting with the scalpel. The engineer must have done the correct calculations for the bridge to carry the traffic load. The accountant has to be certain that the books are accurate in order to have the money to pay the expenses. The skydiver has to know the parachute is folded correctly and will open smoothly.

There are some things in life where you just have to be sure, because the consequences of being wrong are so serious. Christianity is like that. Strangely enough the question "Who is Jesus?" is one many people never bother with, but it's a question which requires careful and clear thinking. It's one which we have to get right.

We discovered in Study 2 that knowledge of Jesus gives us everything we need for life and godliness. Knowledge of Jesus equips a person to negotiate life wisely. It's through a knowledge of Jesus that we participate in the divine nature as God's own Spirit resides in us, changing us and leading us to become more like Jesus.

Knowledge of Jesus is no small thing and so it's critical that we gain a *correct* knowledge of Jesus. A wrong knowledge of Jesus will leave you up an eternal river without a paddle.

In this next section of his letter, Peter puts forward two good reasons why our knowledge of Jesus is right.

Investigate

Read 1:12-18

1. How can you tell that Peter considers knowledge of Jesus to be an important thing?

2. How do we know that Peter did not "follow cleverly invented stories"?

3. The incident that Peter is referring to in verses 17-18 is recorded in Mark 9:2-8. Read it now. Why do you think this made such an impression on Peter?

4. *Read Luke 1:1-4.* What intentions do Luke and Peter have in common?

The testimony of eyewitnesses

"I saw it with my own eyes."

There is nothing quite like eyewitness testimony to bring you in close to an event. There were eyewitnesses who met Jesus, and Peter was one of them.

Peter saw and heard that Jesus was God's Son in the flesh. So important is that knowledge that Peter wanted to spend the rest of his life telling people about it.

We, also, should feel the force of this argument. Jesus is not just a nice character in a nice story. He is not in the same category as Mother Goose or Rudolph the red-nosed reindeer. Jesus is an historical person whom eyewitnesses wrote about. This reality gives us a solid foundation for trusting in him.

Investigate

Read 1:19-21

1. What is the meaning of verse 19? (Rev 22:16 may help.)

2. What further reason does Peter give in these verses for having confidence in our knowledge of Jesus?

3. How does Peter's understanding of Scripture compare with Paul's from 2 Timothy 3:14-17?

The testimony of the prophets

We can be certain of our knowledge of Jesus not only because it comes from eyewitnesses, but also because of the testimony of the Old Testament prophets who spoke from God. Prophet after prophet looked forward to the day when God would visit this earth. These prophets were spread over hundreds of years of history with some of them being totally unaware of what the others were saying or had said.

Peter's point is that it's no coincidence that all these diverse prophets all predicted the same thing and that Jesus came and perfectly fulfilled all the things they had been talking about. It's no coincidence that it all happened that way, because the Old Testament is God himself telling us about Jesus.

All this should give us great confidence in our knowledge of Jesus. It's a knowledge that comes from God himself, not from people who cooked up clever stories.

Being a confident, clear-minded Christian

We have discovered in our studies so far that Peter is writing to encourage his readers to be clear-minded about what is important and what is not (3:1). In this respect, Peter has stressed that the clear-thinking Christian understands the importance of a knowledge of Jesus Christ (1:3). More than that, Peter says the clear-thinking Christian can also be confident in his or her knowledge of Jesus because it comes from eyewitnesses and from God himself speaking through the prophets.

This is a powerful thought.

We live in a world that doesn't believe in capital 'T' Truth. We live in an age in which nothing is absolute—truth is what happens to suit you. The apostle Peter's teaching lifts the mist of this sort of hazy thinking to show that the Christian faith is founded on clear facts, not fairy stories.

Christianity is not people thinking about God. It is God revealing himself to eyewitnesses. That is surely something to excite us and fill us with a clear and certain belief in Jesus Christ.

Think it through

1. Think about the times you have doubted Christianity. What has been causing these doubts? How can 2 Peter 1:16-21 help you at these times?

2. Are there other things which Peter doesn't mention which you feel have led you to have a confidence in your knowledge of Jesus?

3. Peter has a very high opinion of Scripture. Do you share his opinion, especially in regard to the Old Testament? How might this show in your lifestyle?

The surprising virtue of intolerance

"I just can't believe this sort of thing is in the Bible."

"It's so harsh, so narrow-minded, so intolerant!"

"How on earth could anyone write this and claim to be Christian. Jesus would never say these sorts of things."

These are some of the reactions people have to 2 Peter 2. It is certainly not the part of the Bible most likely to appear on a poster with alpine scenes.

2 Peter 2 concerns a situation so disastrous that some straight talking is required, irrespective of who it upsets or offends or embarrasses. This chapter concerns such a disaster that it is impossible to remain calm about it.

The disaster is that certain false teachers are spreading lies about Jesus. That makes Peter angry. Peter is passionate when false teachers peddle a false gospel about Jesus, because he knows that is at stake. People's eternal destinies are being played around with here.

Investigate

Read 2 Peter 2:1-3

1. What can you discover about the content of the heresies being promoted by the false teachers of Peter's day?

2. How might heresies be "secretly" (v.1) introduced?

3. Peter says that many will follow the false prophets (v.2). Glance over the remainder of the chapter to see if you can discover any reasons why these false teachers might be so popular?

The false teachers: their beliefs

The particular false teachers that Peter has in mind here are characterised by their beliefs. Firstly, Peter says that they are denying the sovereign Lord (v.1). The key word here is sovereign. These are people who deny that Jesus has the right to rule our lives.

It is unlikely that the false teachers were coming straight out and telling people to forget about what Jesus says. If they did that, they probably wouldn't get to square one in most churches. But Peter also says in verse 1 that they are *secretly* introducing destructive heresies. This is an undercover job. They are not denying Jesus outright but, nevertheless, the effect of their teaching is to undermine Jesus' authority.

Interestingly, Peter goes on to say that such teachers may well be very popular. They are successful because they are saying things that people want to hear (v.18). False teachers may well be the leaders of large and growing churches.

All this is a warning to us to examine our motives for attending Christian gatherings. Are we drawn to them for reasons other than the truth of Jesus? Are we secretly being led into falsehood, destruction and "shameful ways"? Are our teachers greedily exploiting us (v.20)?

We might also be taken in by more subtle falsehoods. Is your church focussing on something other than the truth of Christ: social appearances? great music? denominational loyalty? Any number of things might lead us away from the truth of our sovereign Lord. That would be diabolical.

Investigate

Read 2 Peter 2:4-22*

1. What does Peter say about the fate of these false teachers?

2. In these verses, Peter reminds his readers of several Old Testament incidents. If you are unfamiliar with any of them it would be helpful to look them up and read them. (You will find the story of Noah in Genesis 6-9; Sodom and Gomorrah and Lot's story in Genesis 19; and Balaam in Numbers 22.) How do each of these incidents add force to Peter's argument?

3. What impressions are you left with after reading 2 Peter 2?

*Note: vv. 10b-11 are difficult, both to translate and to interpret. The original recipients of the letter evidently had the appropriate background knowledge to understand what Peter was referring to exactly, but it is very difficult for us to know with any certainty. See Michael Green's Tyndale commentary for a good summary of the various possibilities. Fortunately, the verses are not integral to the argument of the chapter as a whole.

The false teachers: their fate and true nature

Peter is uncompromising in his description of the false teachers. The false teachers are described as abusive, slanderous, unreasoning dreamers. They are wicked, stupid people with less spirituality than apes. They promise much, but they can deliver nothing. They are froth and bubble with no substance.

It's a savage word picture, but it doesn't even end there. In a series of "if" statements, Peter refers us back to the way God has dealt with sin in the Old Testament (vv.4-9). Peter's conclusion is that there will come a time when such false teachers will face the full fury of God. 'Gentle Jesus meek and mild' will reward them with eternal punishment.

It's at this point that some people get upset because this all seems too hard, too unloving, too intolerant. But we need to think about the seriousness of what the false teachers are doing. They may be really nice, friendly people, but they are also very dangerous because they are giving people a false gospel and a false assurance about eternal life.

Consider the outcry when a medical doctor gets it wrong and a patient is misdiagnosed. Consider the outcry when a politician makes a mistake in Parliament and everyone is screaming for his or her resignation. Consider the outcry that *should* go up when a Bible teacher gets it wrong and people never hear the true gospel.

Investigate

Re-read 2 Peter 2:20-22

1. In these verses, Peter describes the condition of those people who come under the influence of false teachings and are led away from Jesus. What effect can these false teachers have on people?

2. What things do you think we can do to help prevent people drifting away from Jesus?

The truth of falsehood

As we've discovered, this chapter concludes with a very passionate warning. Nothing can be more serious than someone teaching false things about Jesus, because it affects the eternal destinies of people. That is why Peter gets so angry about false teachers who are luring people away from Jesus. They are, in effect, luring people to hell. When that's happening, it's not the time to sit back and be polite. It's far too serious for that.

What we are discovering over and over again in 2 Peter is the sheer importance of our knowledge of Jesus. A true knowledge of Jesus can give us a place in the Kingdom of God. A false knowledge of Jesus is, therefore, disastrous.

The spirit of this age says that everything is relative, especially in the area of religion. If something works for you, that's considered great—but something different may work for me. Everything is considered right in its own way. 'Tolerance' is the buzz word. To be intolerant of anything is to be narrow and bigoted.

But sometimes you have to be intolerant. I am intolerant of my daughter playing with sharp knives. Society is intolerant of drunk drivers. Sometimes being intolerant is the most loving thing you can be. We should be intolerant of people who teach a false knowledge of Jesus. The truth is that some things are false.

Think it through

1. Do you think this chapter is too severe and uncompromising? Why or why not?

2. How can we guard ourselves against falling victim to false teachers?

3. How can we help others whom we think are being influenced by false teachers?

Does God wear a wristwatch?

Several years ago a leading news magazine ran a story about the second coming of Jesus. The magazine gathered a team of marketing experts to plan how Jesus should be promoted when he does come back. Public relations directors were asked what advice they would give to Jesus in order to ensure that his return visit would be a success. This advice included:

> The new Jesus must come across as action orientated. He must be perceived as a Leader, able to deliver. Therefore, He should participate in a sport that helps profile those qualities... I think tennis is just right for Jesus.
>
> He can still dress in white, television coverage is guaranteed and the corporate sector will really identify with Him. Tennis also gives Jesus a chance to perform some miracles. Twenty aces in a row, that sort of thing.
>
> *The Bulletin*, September 12, 1989

In the final chapter of 2 Peter, God explains what Jesus' return *will* be like and it's interesting to note the different perspective. Whereas the magazine article was full of ideas about what *Jesus* will have to do when he comes back, God is much more interested in telling us what *we* have to do in order to get ready for Jesus.

That's a big difference. Jesus is the important one, not us! When Jesus comes back it won't be a matter of him changing to suit us—it'll be a matter of whether or not we have changed to suit him. This perspective dominates the last chapter of 2 Peter.

Before Peter can get to the specifics, there are some initial problems that need to be cleared up.

Investigate

Read 2 Peter 3:1-4

1. What specific problem is Peter now addressing in his letter?

2. Why do the scoffers think that Jesus will not be back?

3. Do you think this is still a problem today? Have you encountered it?

A denial

In the last study we saw that Peter was angry with the presence of false teachers who were secretly introducing lies about Jesus. As Peter now turns to deal with one of those lies, we can almost hear their voices: "It's been years since Jesus died. If he was coming back he'd be back by now. Life just goes on. He won't be back!".

You can still see this same scoffing in things like the magazine article mentioned above. Certainly, the article was intended as a bit of fun, but underlying it all is the idea that it will never happen. The whole notion of Jesus coming back is just not taken seriously. It's been 2000 years since Jesus' birth and his return is so unlikely that the topic can be treated with contempt.

Peter responds to this scoffing with two main arguments.

Investigate

Read 2 Peter 3:5-7

1. What is Peter's point here?

2. How effective an argument do you think this is against the scoffers?

Argument 1: God is faithful

Peter affirms that Jesus' will return because of the certainty of God's Word. If God says he's going to do something, he will do it. So powerful is God that he made the world with just a word. More than that, God has already judged the world once before in the time of Noah and nothing can stop him from judging the world again.

This argument gathers great force when we consider that, unlike us, God is completely sovereign. When I go out to a meeting, many things can prevent me from returning home at the time I promised my wife. The meeting might run over time, the car can break down or my train can be delayed. That sort of thing happens to us all the time, because much of life is outside our control.

Nothing is outside God's control. He made the world and nothing can make God late for an appointment. God has said that Jesus will come back and God doesn't make promises he can't keep.

But this raises a question. If nothing can stop Jesus from coming back, why hasn't he? What's the hold up? Could it have slipped God's mind? Peter answers that question in verses 8-9.

Investigate

Read 2 Peter 3:8-10

1. What do you think is Peter's main point in verse 8?

2. What reason does Peter give for Jesus not yet coming back?

3. Jesus' return will come like a thief (v.10). What does this mean?

4. What will happen when Jesus does come back ?

Argument 2: God is merciful

To us, two thousand years seems a long time. It's not to God. All the way through this letter, Peter has been broadening our perspective to take in God's eternal perspective. Within an eternal time frame, two thousand years is the blink of an eye.

Indeed, God isn't very interested in time. God doesn't wear a wristwatch—time is not the thing that matters to him. What does matter to God is people. God is merciful. He is holding off Jesus' return so that people might repent.

God isn't interested in getting Jesus back as fast as possible so as to punish as many people as possible. It's not like one of those games of hide and seek where the person counts as fast as they possibly can so that no-one has time to hide! No—God is concerned for people and he is patiently holding back judgement to give people a chance to get ready.

This brings us to the next logical step. If God is delaying his return in order to give people a chance to respond to the gospel, what do you think God would like us to be doing during this time of delay?

God doesn't want anyone to perish and neither should we. Perhaps there is someone you need to talk to about Jesus before it's too late. For we must not forget, even though God is merciful in delaying his judgement, he nevertheless has appointed a day when we will all have to give account. The day of the Lord *will* come like a thief in the night.

Think it through

1. How much do you think about Jesus' return? Do you believe he will come back? How does this show in your life?

2. Read 1 Thessalonians 5:1-11. What insights do these verses add concerning Jesus' return?

3. Jesus really is going to return: how should this affect our evangelism?

4. Make a short list of people whom you want to tell about Jesus. Pray specifically for them and ask for opportunities to share the gospel with them before Jesus comes back!

6

Go ahead, make God's day

A few years ago, Queen Elizabeth II came to visit the country town where I live. It was the second time she had come to the town and a huge fuss was made. Flowers suddenly appeared along the route she was to take. Trees were pruned to look all nice and neat. Lawns were mown, streets resurfaced, buildings were cleaned and painted. A lot of people went to a lot of trouble so that the town was ready for the Queen's second visit.

How will we get ready for Jesus' return on his second visit? It will be a day when the entire fabric of creation will be dissolved and a whole new order of creation, a new heaven and a new earth will be ushered in. What do we need to do to get ready for that? How can we be prepared?

Investigate

Read 2 Peter 3:11-18

1. What should we be doing to get ready for Jesus' return?

2. What do you think it means to "live holy and godly lives" (v. 11)? (These cross references may help: 2 Cor 7:1; 1 Pet 2:9-12; 1 Thess 4:1-7.)

3. In verse 14 we are told to "make every effort to be found spotless, blameless and at peace with him" and in verse 18 to "grow in the grace and knowledge" of Jesus. In chapter 1, Peter told us to make every effort to work out our salvation. How are these commands related?

Be holy!

When Jesus returns he will see us for who we really are. Being ready for Jesus, therefore, is a matter of working at our holiness.

Notice that Peter calls on us to be "holy", not "busy". We might be very busy doing many things around our church or fellowship group, but are we actually making the effort to be holy in all our activities?

But how do we become holy? What can we be doing in practical terms to grow in holiness? Peter gives some wise advice.

Investigate

1. What does Peter suggest his readers do in 3:1-2? How might this help them to grow in godliness?

2. Why do you think Peter suddenly starts talking about the apostle Paul here? What is Peter's main point in verses 15-16?

3. Given what Peter has already said about Scripture (1:20-21), why is it significant that he refers to Paul's writings as Scripture?

4. Even Peter could see that some of Paul's writings were hard to understand! How can we approach difficult Bible passages in such a way that we don't distort them?

How to be holy

The final chapter of 2 Peter sets out some helpful advice about how we can live holy lives.

Recall Scripture

Peter's first advice about growing in holiness returns to verses 1-2. Peter urges us to have wholesome thinking by recalling Scripture.

One reason we all have problems trying to be holy is because we can't be bothered reading the Bible. We buy a newspaper or our favourite magazine and we read it from cover to cover, but the Bible just sits by our bedside. No wonder we find it difficult to be blameless in our lives. We fill our minds with trivia and it comes out in our lives. We fill our heads with magazines and novels and television, but not with the Word of God. The end result is that we crave the world and not the Word.

If we're serious about getting ready for Jesus, we'll be training our minds in wholesome thinking by recalling and reading and thinking over Scripture.

Guard against error

Peter's second piece of practical advice about how to live a holy life is that we should be on our guard against errors. Peter has already spent the entire second chapter on this topic. In chapter 3, Peter talks to his readers about this in terms of Paul's letters (vv.15-16).

He points out that some people are distorting Paul's words. Some of what Paul says is hard to understand and so we need to be careful. We need to treat the Bible with respect and not embrace ideas too quickly, especially when the Bible itself doesn't seem to be black and white on an issue.

This is yet another reason for knowing the Scriptures. If we are not well acquainted with what the Bible says, we will be easily fooled by false teachers. More to the point, if we don't know what's in the Bible we'll be incapable of living holy and godly lives simply because we won't know what a holy and godly life involves.

Grow

Thirdly, Peter says that holy living will involve growing in the grace and knowledge of Jesus Christ (v.18). The key word in the verse is "grow". We should never think that we've 'arrived' as Christians. The Christian life is a developing life consisting of getting to know, at ever greater depth, an inexhaustible Lord and Saviour. We must always be striving to know Jesus more fully.

Knowledge of Jesus

We've now reached the end of our journey through 2 Peter. It's a challenging and comforting letter. It's also no accident that the final verse in the letter takes us full circle back to the start.

Knowledge of Jesus is Peter's opening (1:2-3) and closing emphasis (3:18). It is the issue around which the whole letter revolves. Knowledge of Jesus gives us everything we need for life and godliness (1:3) and it is therefore critical in helping us grow in godliness so that we might be ready for Jesus' return (3:11). Furthermore, because knowledge of Jesus is so important, people who promote false knowledge must not be tolerated (2:1-22).

From start to finish, 2 Peter is all about Jesus and how crucial it is to accurately know him. No wonder Peter wants to spend his last dying day telling people about Jesus (1:12-15).

Think it through

1. Are you growing in the grace and knowledge of Christ? If not, how does 2 Peter 3 help you to do so? If so, how can you ensure that the growth continues?

2. What are some areas in your life that need work if you are to be spotless for when Jesus returns? What are some ways that you can really improve these problem areas? Be specific.

3. Think back over all of 2 Peter. What are the things that have comforted you the most?

4. What are the things that have challenged you the most?

Who are we?

Ever since we opened our doors in 1991 in the UK as St Matthias Press, our aim has been to provide the Christian community with products of a uniformly high standard—both in their biblical faithfulness and in the quality of the writing and production.

Now known asThe Good Book Company, we have grown to become an international provider of user-friendly resources, with Christians of all sorts using our Bible studies, books, Briefings, audio cassettes, videos, training courses and events.

Buy direct from us and save

If you order your resources direct from us, you can not only save time and money, you invest in more great resources for the future:

- you save time—we usually despatch our orders within 24 hours of receiving them
- you save money—if you order in bulk, you'll save even more
- you help keep us afloat—because we get more from each sale, buying from us direct helps us to stay alive and develop new Biblical resources for the future.

Please call us for a free catalogue of all our resources, including an up-to-date list of other titles in this Interactive Bible Studies series. Some details of IBS titles are contained on the following page.

Audio Tapes

We also have available audio tapes of the sermon series upon which this set of studies are based. 10 tapes. Call us to order the series.

| ☎ (020) 8942-0880 | ✉ PO Box 665, London SW20 8RL | FAX (020) 8942-0990 (pay by credit card or invoice) |

Email: admin@thegoodbook.co.uk
Website: www.thegoodbook.co.uk

MORE GREAT RESOURCES FROM THE GOOD BOOK COMPANY

Interactive Bible Studies

Our Interactive Bible Studies (IBS) and Topical Bible Studies (TBS) are a valuable resource to help you keep feeding from God's Word. The IBS series works through passages and books of the Bible; the TBS series pulls together the Bible's teaching on topics, such as money or prayer. As at July 2000, the series contains the following titles:

BEYOND EDEN
(GENESIS 1-11)
Authors: Phillip Jensen
and Tony Payne, 9 studies

THE ONE AND ONLY
(DEUTERONOMY)
Author: Bryson Smith,
8 studies

FAMINE & FORTUNE
(RUTH)
Authors: Barry Webb &
David Hohne, 4 studies

THE EYE OF THE STORM
(JOB)
Author: Bryson Smith,
6 studies

TWO CITIES
(ISAIAH)
Authors: Andrew Reid and
Karen Morris, 9 studies

KINGDOM OF DREAMS
(DANIEL)
Authors: Andrew Reid and
Karen Morris, 8 studies

BURNING DESIRE
(OBADIAH & MALACHI)
Authors: Phillip Jensen and
Richard Pulley, 6 studies

FULL OF PROMISE
(THE BIG PICTURE OF THE O.T.)
Authors: Phil Campbell
& Bryson Smith, 8 studies

THE GOOD LIVING GUIDE
(MATTHEW 5:1-12)
Authors: Phillip Jensen
and Tony Payne, 9 studies

NEWS OF THE HOUR
(MARK)
Author: Peter Bolt,
10 studies

FREE FOR ALL
(GALATIANS)
Authors: Phillip Jensen
& Kel Richards, 8 studies

WALK THIS WAY
(EPHESIANS)
Author: Bryson Smith,
8 studies

THE COMPLETE CHRISTIAN
(COLOSSIANS)
Authors: Phillip Jensen
and Tony Payne, 8 studies

ALL LIFE IS HERE
(1 TIMOTHY)
Authors: Phillip Jensen
and Greg Clarke, 9 studies

THE PATH TO GODLINESS
(TITUS)
Authors: Phillip Jensen
and Tony Payne, 6 studies

THE IMPLANTED WORD
(JAMES)
Authors: Phillip Jensen
and K.R. Birkett, 8 studies

HOMEWARD BOUND
(1 PETER)
Authors: Phillip Jensen
and Tony Payne, 10 studies

ALL YOU NEED TO KNOW
(2 PETER)
Author: Bryson Smith,
6 studies

BOLD I APPROACH
(PRAYER)
Author: Tony Payne,
6 studies

CASH VALUES
(MONEY)
Author: Tony Payne,
5 studies

THE BLUEPRINT
(DOCTRINE)
Authors: Phillip Jensen
& Tony Payne, 11 studies